I love reading

Blast Off!
by Ruth Owen

Editorial consultant: Mitch Cronick

ticktock

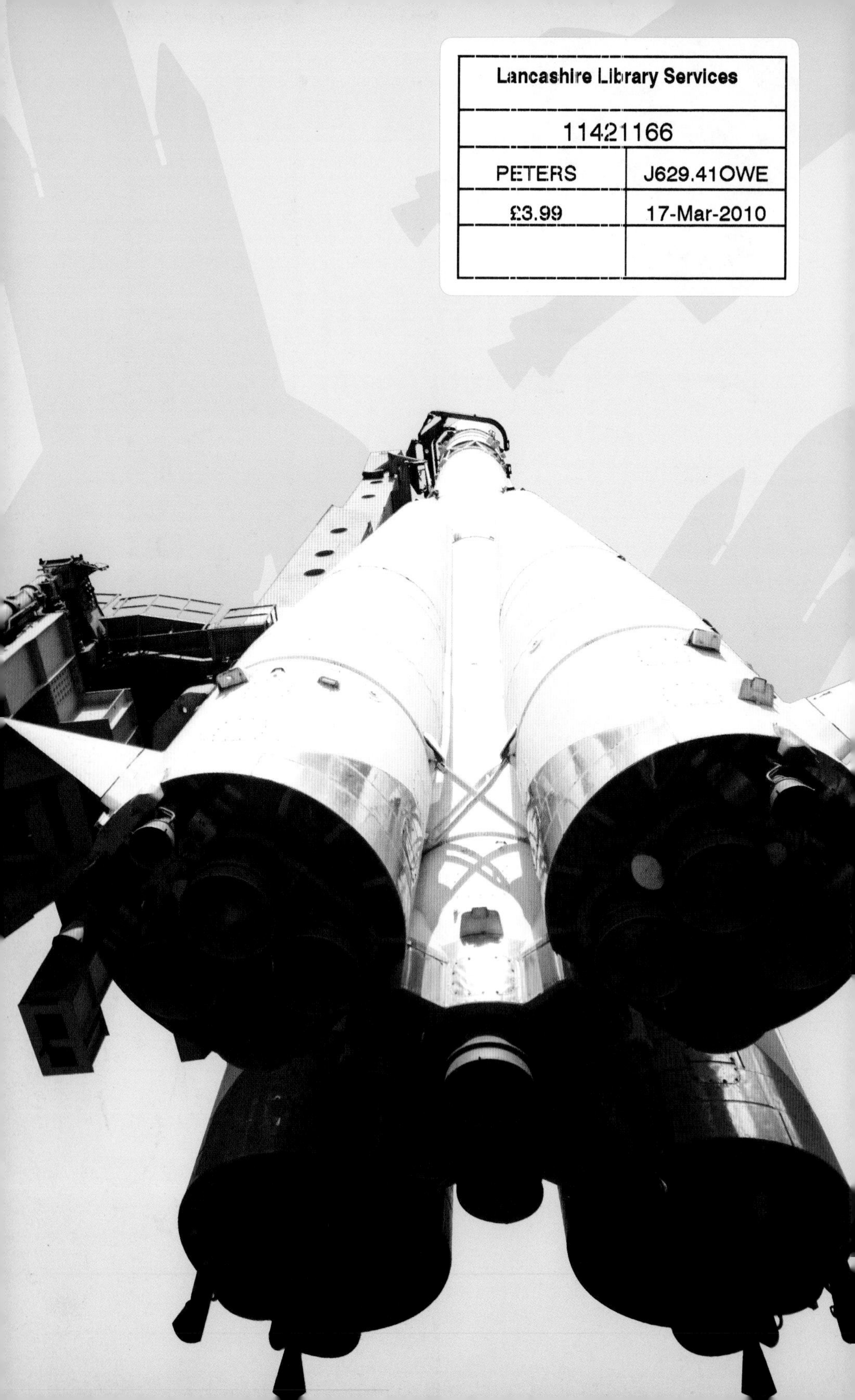

CONTENTS

Words in **bold** are explained in the glossary.

Blast off!

Five...

Four...

Three...

4

Rocket

Space shuttle

Two...
One...
Blast off!

5

Let's go!

The **space shuttle** goes into **space**.

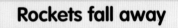

Rockets fall away

6

Look at the astronauts

The **astronauts** ride in the space shuttle.

Helmet

Astronaut

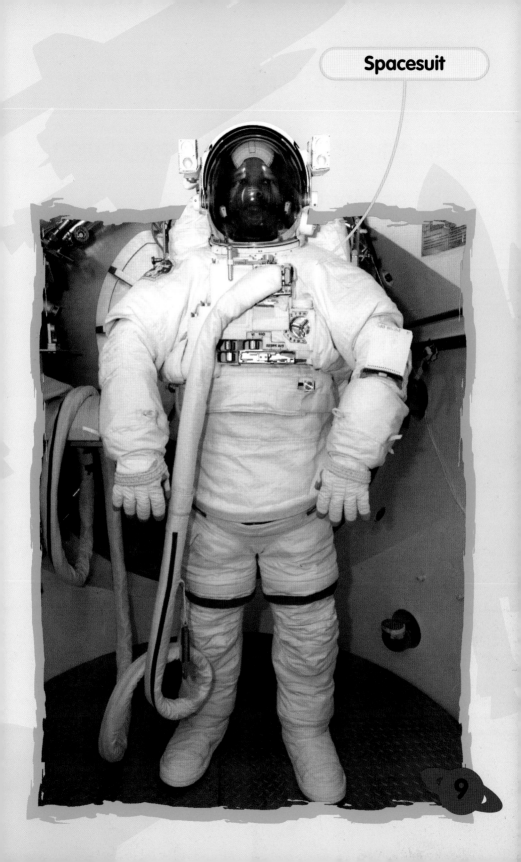

Spacesuit

The space station

The shuttle goes to the **space station**.

The astronauts work here.

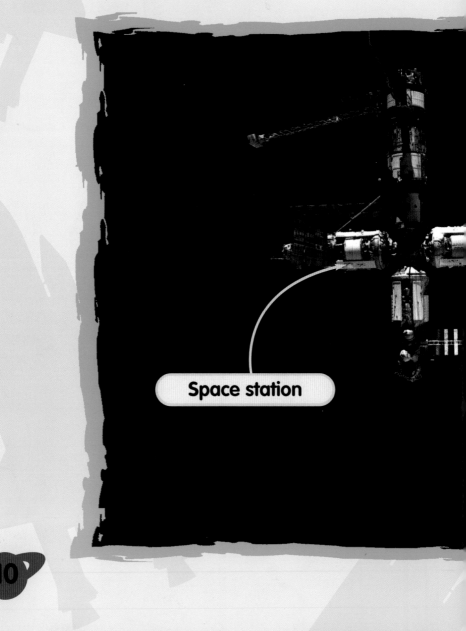

Space station

Astronaut

Shuttle

11

What can we see?

There is a lot to see in space.

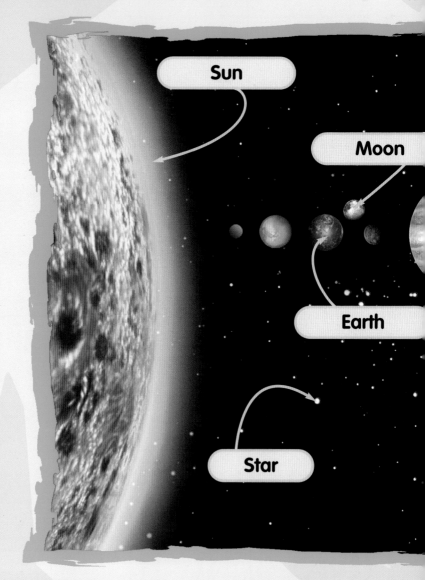

Our planet

We live on a **planet** called Earth.

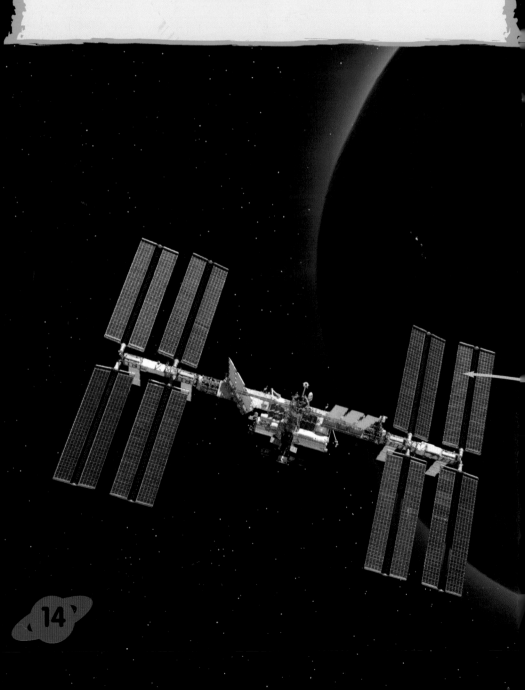

Earth

Space station

'15

The Moon

We can see the Moon at night.

Star

Moon

Earth

'17

On the Moon

Some astronauts have been to the Moon!

Spaceship

Astronaut

Look at Mars!

This planet is
called Mars.

Earth

Mars

Astronauts will go to Mars one day.

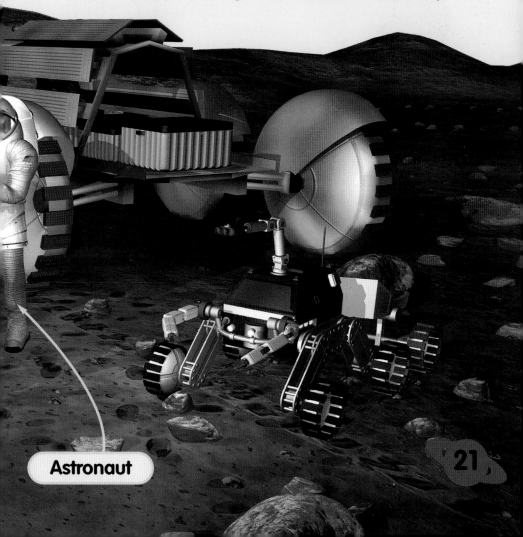

Astronaut

Glossary

astronaut
A person who goes into space.

planet
A large round object in space. Earth and Mars are planets.

space
Everything away from our Earth. There are stars and planets in space.

space shuttle

A spaceship that is blasted into space on a rocket. It flies back to Earth like a plane.

space station

A very big spaceship where astronauts work. They find out about space and our Earth.

23

Index

Publisher: Melissa Fairley
Studio Manager: Sara Greasley
Editor: Emma Dods
Designer: Trudi Webb
Production Controller: Ed Green
Production Manager: Suzy Kelly

ISBN: 978 1 84898 114 0

Printed in China
9 8 7 6 5 4 3 2 1

A CIP catalogue record for this book is available from the British Library. All rights reserved. No part of this publication may be reproduced, copied, stored in a retrieval system or transmitted in any form or by any means electronic, mechanical, photocopying, recording or otherwise without prior written permission of the copyright owner.

Picture credits (t=top, b=bottom, c=centre, l=left, r=right, OFC=outside front cover, OBC=outside back cover):
Nasa: 14. Nasa/courtesy of nasaimages.org: OFCl, 1, 4–5, 6b, 6l, 8, 9, 10, 18, 19, 21t, 23b, 22l. Nasa/JPL: 20–21.
Shutterstock: OFC background, 2, 6–7, 11t, 11b, 14–15 main, 16-17 all, 22r, 23t, OBC. Ticktock Media Archive: 12–13.

Every effort has been made to trace the copyright holders, and we apologize in advance for any unintentional omissions.
We would be pleased to insert the appropriate acknowledgements in any subsequent edition of this publication.